Albert Einstein

by Dana Meachen Rau

Compass Point Early Biographies

Content Adviser: Alice Calaprice, author and editor of The Quotable Einstein
and senior editor, Princeton University Press, Princeton, New Jersey

Reading Adviser: Dr. Linda D. Labbo,
Department of Reading Education, College of Education,
The University of Georgia

COMPASS POINT BOOKS

Minneapolis, Minnesota

Compass Point Books
3109 West 50th Street, #115
Minneapolis, MN 55410

Visit Compass Point Books on the Internet at *www.compasspointbooks.com*
or e-mail your request to *custserv@compasspointbooks.com*

Photographs ©: Hulton/Archive by Getty Images, cover, 14, 18 (bottom), 19, 25; PhotoDisc,
cover background; Courtesy of the Albert Einstein Archives, The Jewish National & University
Library, The Hebrew University of Jerusalem, Israel, 3 (top & middle), 7, 8, 9, 10, 12, 13 (top);
Stock Montage, 3 (bottom), 4, 6, 20; Hulton-Deutsch Collection/Corbis, 11; Underwood &
Underwood/Corbis, 13 (bottom), 18 (top), 24; Bettmann/Corbis, 16, 17, 21, 22; TimePix, 26.

Editors: E. Russell Primm, Emily J. Dolbear, and Catherine Neitge
Photo Researcher: Svetlana Zhurkina
Photo Selector: Linda S. Koutris
Designer/Page Production: Bradfordesign, Inc./Erin Scott, SARIN creative

Library of Congress Cataloging-in-Publication Data
Rau, Dana Meachen, 1971–
 Albert Einstein / by Dana Rau.
  p. cm. — (Compass Point early biographies)
Contents: Wonder about the world—Albert's childhood—His favorite subjects—Work and
marriage—New ideas—A famous man—A peaceful world—Man of the century—Important
dates in Einstein's life.
 ISBN 0-7565-0416-3 (hardcover)
 ISBN 0-7565-1050-3 (paperback)
 1. Einstein, Albert, 1879–1955—Juvenile literature. 2. Physicists—Biography—Juvenile literature. [1. Einstein, Albert, 1879–1955. 2. Physicists. 3. Scientists.] I. Title. II. Series.
 QC16.E5 R35 2003
 530'.092—dc21   2002009829

Table of Contents

*Note: In this book, words that are defined in the glossary are in **bold** the first time they appear in the text.*

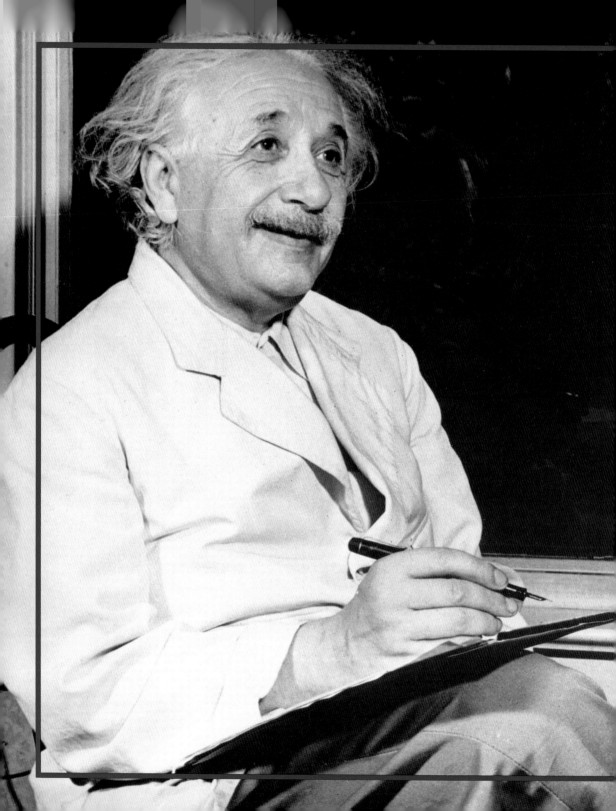

Wonder About the World

Have you ever wondered how the world works? A scientist named Albert Einstein always wondered about that. He thought the world was an amazing place. He was interested in the huge objects found in outer space as well as the tiny bits of matter that can be seen only through a **microscope**. He had many new ideas, or **theories**, about the way the world works. He looked at the world in a way no one else ever had.

◀ Albert Einstein was a scientist who studied how the world works.

Albert's Childhood

Albert Einstein was born on March 14, 1879, in Ulm, Germany. The following year, his parents, Hermann and Pauline Einstein, moved the family to the large city of Munich.

Albert's sense of wonder began when he was a young boy. He liked quiet games that needed a lot of thought, such as building with blocks or making houses of cards.

When Albert was

Young Albert and his family moved to Munich, Germany, when he was one year old.

five years old, his father showed him a compass. A compass is an instrument with a needle that shows the four directions— north, south, east, and west. People use it to show them which way they are going. Ein-

Einstein was a quiet and thoughtful boy.

stein was fascinated by the way the compass moved. The needle always pointed north no matter how he turned the compass. It made him think the world does not always work the way we expect it to.

Favorite Subjects

Albert and his younger sister, Maja

His parents sent Albert and his younger sister, Maja, to a German school. Albert did not like school, though. He thought the teachers were too strict. They always wanted the children to remember a lot of facts. Albert had trouble memorizing words. He felt more comfortable with numbers and ideas. He once

8

said, "Imagination is more important than knowledge."

He did not do well on tests, either. He got good grades only in his favorite subjects—math and science. Albert knew so much about these

Einstein's childhood interest in math and science continued to grow as he became an adult.

subjects that sometimes his teachers did not know the answers to his questions. He studied math and science outside of school, too. His favorite book to read at home was a math book given to him when he was twelve.

Albert Einstein at the Cantonal School in Aarau, Switzerland, shortly before he graduated

Albert left school when he was only fifteen because he disliked it so much. He later earned a diploma from a school in Switzerland. He liked this school a lot and got good grades there. His grades were good enough to continue studying at a **university**. In 1896, Albert began to study **physics** at a university in Zurich, Switzerland. Just as in grade school,

10

Einstein studied physics in ➤ Zurich, beginning in 1896.

Albert never liked going to classes or taking tests. He still worked hard, though. He graduated four years later.

Work and Marriage

Einstein worked in an office before he became a professor.

Einstein wanted to be a **professor**, but he could not find work. So, he took an office job in 1902. He had a lot of extra time to study physics on his own.

In 1903, he married Mileva Maric. She was a woman he had studied with at the university. Together they had two sons. Hans

Mileva Maric and her two sons

Albert was born in 1904 and Eduard was born in 1910. In 1919, Einstein and Mileva divorced. Then Einstein married his cousin, Elsa Löwenthal. She already had two daughters.

Einstein with his second wife, Elsa Löwenthal

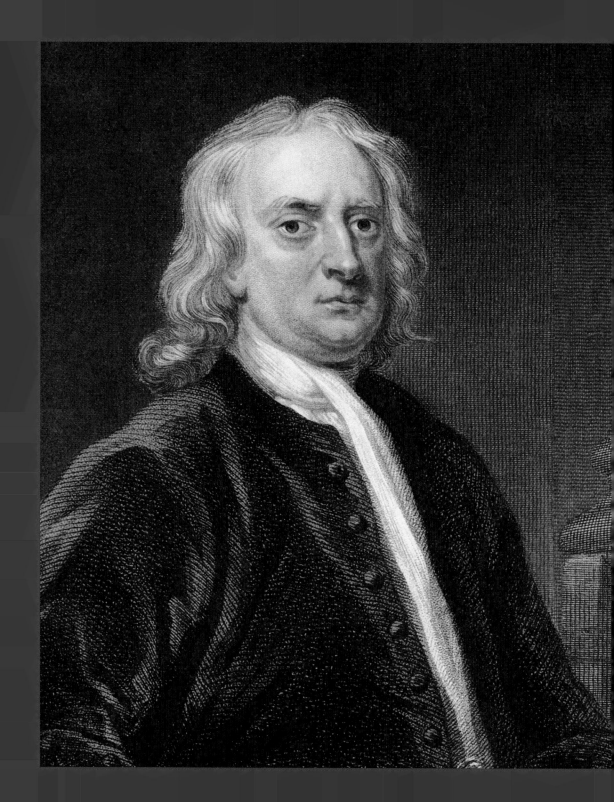

New Ideas

In 1905, Einstein wrote many papers about his theories of how the world works. His most famous paper changed science forever. He introduced the theory of relativity.

Since the 1600s, people had believed in the ideas of a scientist named Sir Isaac Newton. Newton said that space and time never change. He said nature had certain laws that are never broken. People were used to this view of the world.

Einstein had a completely different idea. He believed that space and time do change. He studied energy and the speed of light. He

◄ Sir Isaac Newton, a scientist from the 1600s, had many ideas about the laws of how the world works. Einstein's theories were very different from Newton's.

found that objects change depending on how fast they are moving.

A Famous Man

Einstein's ideas made him famous. He became a professor of physics in the European cities of Zurich

Einstein became a physics professor at several well-known universities.

and Prague. In 1914, he moved to Germany to become a professor at the University of Berlin. He continued his research there but did not teach classes.

In 1921, Einstein was given a special award—the Nobel Prize in physics. Now

◄ Einstein (third from right) was often interviewed by reporters because the world was interested in his ideas about time and space.

Because of his fame and popularity, Einstein was asked to give many lectures.

people all over the world knew about Einstein and his ideas. They wrote articles about him and took photos of him for many newspapers. Even when he became famous, though, Einstein was still a simple man. He

Einstein playing his violin

said, "A table, a chair, a bowl of fruit and a violin;

what else does a man need to be happy."

◀ Einstein (second from right) stands
with fellow Nobel prize winners.

19

A Peaceful World

Einstein cared deeply for the world he wondered about so much. He wanted everyone in the world to live in peace. Einstein was a **pacifist**. He did not believe in war.

Einstein (center) talking with other professors at Princeton University in 1933

In the 1930s, Adolf Hitler was the leader in Germany. He wanted to make Germany a bigger nation by going to war. Hitler also hated Jewish people. He wanted to kill all the

◄ As Adolf Hitler and his government grew stronger, Jewish Germans, including Einstein, left their homeland. Many who did not leave were killed.

21

Jews in Europe. Einstein was Jewish. He did not like what was happening in Germany, so Einstein went to America in 1933. He was given a job as a professor in Princeton, New Jersey.

Einstein did not like war, but he knew other countries would have to fight the Germans to stop Hitler. World War II (1939–1945) finally put an end to Hitler and his hateful policies. For the rest of his life, Einstein spoke out against weapons and war. He believed that people could find peace only by trying to understand one another.

◀ Einstein spoke not only about science, but also about the need for world peace and understanding.

Man of the Century

Albert Einstein spent the rest of his life in Princeton, where he continued to do re-search. He died on April 18, 1955. He was seventy-six years old.

All his life, Einstein was fasci-nated by the way

A front-page article reporting the death of Albert Einstein

the world worked. He used his imagination to form his scientific ideas. And he wished that the world would be a peaceful place. He once said, "Only a life lived for others is a life

◀ Albert Einstein's ideas changed the scientific world and also taught people to question and think about how the world works.

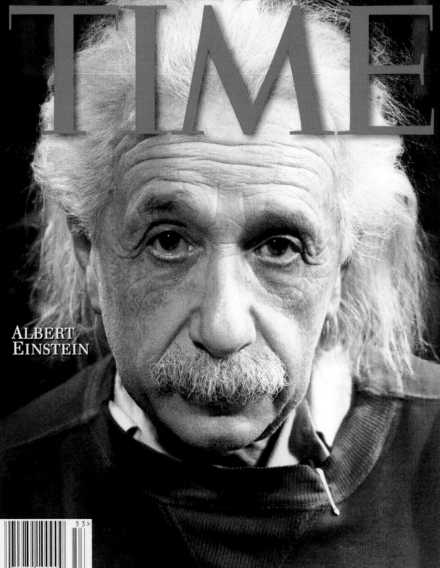

DECEMBER 31, 1999 $4.95

www.time.com

PERSON OF THE CENTURY

TIME

ALBERT
EINSTEIN

Display Until 1/10/00

worthwhile."

Some people have called Einstein the most important person of the twentieth century. He changed the world with his ideas. He taught people how to wonder.

◄ On December 31, 1999, *Time* magazine named Albert Einstein Person of the Century.

Important Dates in Albert Einstein's Life

1879	Born in Ulm, Germany, on March 14
1880	Einstein's family moves to Munich, Germany
1861–1865	Attends the Swiss Federal Institute of Technology in Zurich, Switzerland
1902–1909	Works at the Swiss Patent Office in Bern, Switzerland
1905	Five important papers are published, including one on the theory of relativity
1909	Becomes a professor at the University of Zurich in Switzerland
1911	Becomes a professor at the German University in Prague
1912	Becomes a professor at the Swiss Federal Institute of Technology in Zurich
1914	Moves to Berlin to become a professor at the University of Berlin
1917	Becomes director of the Kaiser Wilhelm Institute for Physics in Berlin
1921	Awarded the Nobel Prize in physics
1933	Arrives in the United States
1955	Dies on April 18

Glossary

microscope—an instrument that makes small objects look larger

pacifist—someone who does not believe in fighting or war

physics—the science of matter and energy

professor—a teacher at a college or university

theories—ideas

university—a school of higher education

Did You Know?

- The street where Albert Einstein was born in Ulm, Germany, is now named Einsteinstrasse, which means "Einstein Street" in German.

- Einstein's mother loved music. As a result, Einstein took violin lessons from age six to fourteen. He played the violin most of his life. He also taught himself to play the piano.

- When Einstein died, researchers studied his brain in an effort to understand why he was so smart. They found the part of the brain that deals with math to be larger in Einstein's brain than in the brains of other people.

Want to Know More?

At the Library

Pirotta, Savior. *Albert Einstein*. Austin, Tex.: Raintree/Steck-Vaughn, 2002.

Reid, Struan. *Albert Einstein*. Chicago: Heinemann Library, 2000.

Sullivan, Anne Marie. *Albert Einstein*. Broomall, Pa.: Mason Crest Publishers, 2002.

On the Web

For more information on this topic, use FactHound.

1. Go to *www.facthound*.com
2. Type in this book ID: 0756504163
3. Click on the *Fetch It* button.

FactHound will find the best Web sites for you.

On the Road

The Historical Society of Princeton

Bainbridge House

158 Nassau Street

Princeton, NJ 08542

To see an exhibit about Einstein's life and work in Princeton

The National Academy of Sciences

2001 Wisconsin Avenue, N.W.

Washington, DC 20007

To see the Albert Einstein Memorial Statue by sculptor Robert Berks

Index

About the Author

Dana Meachen Rau is a children's book author, editor, and illustrator. She has written more than seventy-five books, including non-fiction, biographies, early readers, and historical fiction. She is a graduate of Trinity College in Hartford, Connecticut. Dana works from her home office in Burlington, Connecticut, where she lives with her husband, Chris, and children, Charlie and Allison.

DATE DUE			

Emmeet

SHIPS

Jacqueline Dineen

The Bookwright Press
New York · 1988

Topics

All the words that appear
in **bold** are explained in the
glossary on page 30.

First published in the
United States in 1988 by
The Bookwright Press
387 Park Avenue South
New York, NY 10016

First published in 1988 by
Wayland (Publishers) Ltd
61 Western Road, Hove
East Sussex BN3 1JD, England

© Copyright 1988 Wayland (Publishers) Ltd

ISBN 0–531–18212–6

Library of Congress Catalog Card Number: 87–73158

Cover *A sailing ship taking part in
the Tall Ships Race, 1987.*

Phototypeset by
Kalligraphics Ltd, Redhill, Surrey
Printed in
Belgium by
Casterman S.A.

Contents

The First Ships

The first people on earth lived in wandering tribes. They roamed the countryside, hunting animals for food. Sometimes the animals swam across rivers and escaped. The people puzzled over these strange rivers, and they noticed several things about them. One was that they were full of fish, and fish were good to eat. The people could catch fish near the banks, but thought about how much easier it would be

A Brazilian Indian pushes his dugout canoe up the river using a long pole.

if they could go on the water.

Then the people noticed that dead tree trunks and branches floated on the water. This gave them an idea. Perhaps they could float on the tree trunks. These were the first "boats."

Later they realized that if they hollowed out a tree trunk, they could sit inside it, so they began to make "dugout" canoes. At first they paddled with their hands, then they started to use wooden poles or paddles. People still make dugout canoes in some parts of the world such as the rain forests of Africa and South America, where there are plenty of large trees.

People began to improve on these boats. They had to rely on the materials around them. In North America, the Indians made light canoes by stretching tree bark or animal skins over wooden frames. The Inuit still make animal skin canoes called kayaks.

This kind of canoe is called kayak. The Inuit of North America make their kayaks by stretching animal skins over a wooden frame.

These bowl-shaped boats, called coracles, were originally made in Wales.

The ancient Egyptians gathered reeds that grew along the banks of the Nile River. They tied the reeds in bundles and made rafts and canoes. The Peruvians of South America made very light rafts from **balsa** wood. They discovered that if they attached a sail to the raft, the wind would blow it along. This was much easier than paddling. It is thought that the ancient Peruvians sailed across the Pacific Ocean to the South Sea Islands on their rafts.

In ancient Britain, people fished from light, bowl-shaped boats called coracles, which had wickerwork frames covered with animal skins.

Many of these simple boats can be seen in different parts of the world today. You can see that the modern canoe is a very old idea.

Three children in a modern canoe. The design of canoes has not changed much over the years.

Ships for Exploration and Conquest

As time went by, people became more curious about other lands. At first, they paddled their small boats across lakes and rivers to see what was on the other side. Then they became curious about the oceans. What lay across these vast stretches of water? To find out, they needed bigger and stronger ships.

Some of the first people to explore new lands across the sea were the Vikings. In about A.D. 800, the Vikings began building wooden longships, with oars and square sails. They invaded Britain and other European countries, and some people believe they even sailed to North America.

By the fifteenth century, sailors were making long voyages to explore new lands. They drew maps, but they believed that the

This Viking longship is on display in a museum in Norway.

8

world was flat. Gradually, as explorers learned more about the shape of the world, they were able to make accurate maps.

In Portugal, Prince Henry the Navigator started a school where Portuguese explorers could learn more about **navigation** and maps. The Portuguese began to build big sailing ships and Henry's explorers sailed all over the world, looking for new trade routes. In 1488, Bartholomew Diaz explored the coast of Africa and sailed around the Cape of Good Hope. Vasco da Gama sailed around to Kenya and then on to India in 1497. Ferdinand

Above *The first person to sail around the world was Ferdinand Magellan.*

Three of Magellan's five ships being escorted by islanders of the Philippines.

Sir Francis Drake was the first Englishman to sail around the world.

Magellan was the first person to sail around the world. He completed his three-year voyage in 1522.

Christopher Columbus was an Italian who was working for Spain. In 1492, he sailed west to find a new route to India and China, and reached America. The three ships on this voyage were the *Santa Maria*, the *Pinta* and the *Nina*.

Sir Francis Drake, an English sea captain, sailed around the world in the *Golden Hind* from 1577 to 1580. He was the first Englishman to make this voyage.

Nearly 200 years later, another British explorer, Captain James Cook, made three journeys around the world in his sailing ships, H.M.S. *Endeavour* and *Resolution*. He sailed to Australia on his first voyage in 1768.

A cutaway illustration of H.M.S. Endeavour, *the ship used by Captain Cook on his first voyage of exploration to Australia.*

Merchant Ships

Sea trading began in the Mediterranean Sea about 4,000 years ago. The Egyptians exchanged grain and other foods for items they were short of, such as wood from Lebanon. They built long wooden ships with oars and sails. The Phoenicians designed short, broad trading ships with plenty of room for the cargo, which included metals, wine, oils, ivory and honey. The ancient Greeks and the Romans copied this design.

The Arab dhow was the first ship to have the triangular sail that are still used on modern sailboats. The Arabs traded along the coast of Africa. Dhows can still be seen today.

By the seventeenth century, people in Europe knew far more about the world. New trade routes had been discovered, and people

Part of the decoration on this Greek vase shows a merchant ship powered by sail.

wanted spices, silks and other goods they could not buy in Europe. Groups of merchants set up new trading companies. The famous East India Company was started in 1602. Its ships, the stately *East Indiamen*, carried lead, copper and wines to the East and returned with silks, spices, furniture and **porcelain.**

Above *An Arab dhow in full sail. Dhows are still very much in use today.*

At the same time, Europeans were forming new **colonies** in America. They relied on the slow *East Indiamen* to bring them goods from the East. In the nineteenth century, the Americans began to develop fast sailing ships called clippers. The clippers were used to carry people to California during the gold rush of 1849, but the clippers could also transport cargoes more speedily than the *East Indiamen*.

Some clippers brought wool and grain from Australia. Others sailed to China to collect tea, which was

The clipper ship Surprise. *Clippers were much faster than the heavy merchant sailing ships and were used to carry people as well as cargo.*

USS ESSEX

The U.S.S. Essex *was a steamship. It was in use until 1930.*

sold in England and America. One of the fastest clippers, the *Cutty Sark*, could sail from Australia to England in sixty-nine days.

The clipper's main competition was the steamship. Steamships needed fuel, and the early ones were unreliable. They did not really begin to take over until 1870, just after the Suez Canal was opened. The **canal** shortened the journey to Australia and the East, but was not suitable for sailing ships.

The container ship American Ace *laden with cargo stowed in container boxes.*

The big steamships were made of iron until about 1890. Then they were made of steel. Modern cargo ships have **diesel engines** and are made of steel or aluminum. Some of them are huge. Container ships are designed to carry goods in large boxes of the same shape and size. The boxes are loaded and unloaded by cranes, so fewer workers are needed at the ports.

Other cargo ships are built to carry grain. The loose grain is poured into the ships through pipes.

One of the most valuable cargoes today is **crude oil**. The world's largest ships are oil tankers called Very Large Crude Carriers (VLCCs), which can carry thousands of tons of oil at a time.

The supertanker Hercules *waits to pick up oil at Valdez, Alaska.*

Passenger ships

As people learned about lands such as America and Australia, they left Europe and went to live in them. The first settlers traveled on cargo ships. The voyages were slow and uncomfortable. During the nineteenth century, shipbuilders began to develop special passenger ships.

The first passenger ships were the American steamboats, which plied up and down rivers like the Mississippi and the Hudson. These riverboats were fast and efficient, and people enjoyed traveling on them. Some boat owners tried to tempt more passengers by offering the fastest journey. Steamboats raced each other along the rivers. Sometimes they collided or burst their boilers.

What people really wanted were faster ships that could cross the

A passanger steamboat on the Nile River, Egypt.

Atlantic Ocean. In 1837, two steamers, the *Great Western* and the *Sirius*, made the first transatlantic crossings, and in 1840 Samuel Cunard set up the first regular passenger service, the Cunard Line.

Cunard started with three little steamers that were not much more comfortable than the old sailing ships. By 1907, the Cunard Line had luxury liners like the *Mauretania* and the *Lusitania*. Sea travel became more comfortable.

The ocean steamer Great Eastern *had sails, as well as engines to drive its paddle wheels.*

Speed was still very important. Ships tried to beat each other's records for fast Atlantic crossings. The fastest ship won the Blue Riband Trophy. The *Mauretania* held the Blue Riband from 1909 until 1928, when the German liner, *Bremen*, beat the record.

In 1912, the White Star Company tried to beat the record with its new liner, the *Titanic*. The ship hit an iceberg and sank. More than 1,500 people died.

In 1912, the Titanic *was the largest and most luxurious transatlantic liner. Her first journey ended in tragedy when she hit an iceberg and sank.*

Above *The* Queen Mary *in 1945, sailing into New York harbor.*

Right *Today the* Queen Mary *is permanently moored in Los Angeles, where it is used as a luxury hotel.*

The big liners had restaurants, swimming pools, ballrooms, and comfortable cabins. They continued to get faster. By the 1950s it only took three or four days to cross the Atlantic. Liners such as the *Queen Mary*, the *Queen Elizabeth* and the *United States* were like luxurious floating hotels.

Today, people rarely travel by passenger liner. It is far quicker to go by air. Most of the old liners have been broken up or converted into cruise ships. Modern liners such as the *Queen Elizabeth 2* were designed to take people on luxury cruises.

Ferries make regular journeys across stretches of water, carrying passengers and sometimes vehicles.

A modern cruise liner, the Island Princess, *awaits her passengers in Auckland, New Zealand.*

The Boeing Jetfoil, a type of hydrofoil, skims across the surface of the water on wing-like devices.

Modern car ferries have large doors at each end. Cars, buses and trucks are driven on at one end and off at the other.

These ships are not very fast. Two faster kinds of passenger ferries are the hovercraft and the hydrofoil. Both skim across the surface of the water. The hovercraft travels on a cushion of air. The hydrofoil has wing-like devices called foils that lift it out of the water.

Warships

Some of the earliest ships were designed as warships. Trading ships were short and wide for carrying plenty of cargo. Fighting ships were long and narrow to give them speed.

In about 500 B.C., the Phoenicians and the ancient Greeks fought sea battles in longships rowed by slaves. Above the rowers was a fighting deck for the soldiers. Some longships had just one row or "bank" of oarsmen along each side. Larger ships had two, three or five banks, one above the other. These ships were called biremes, triremes or quinqueremes. Most ships had a single sail.

The Romans also used longships, but they were not very suitable for heavy seas. In northern Europe, fighting ships were the same as cargo ships for hundreds of years.

This Greek warship, a bireme, has fifty oars. It has a bronze spike at the front to ram enemy ships.

This painting by Nicholas Hilliard shows a scene from the Armada. In 1588, Spain sent a fleet of galleons to attack England.

In 1588, Spain attacked England with its famous Armada of galleons. These were the same heavy sailing ships that were used to bring treasure back from the **New World**. They had three or four masts and huge square sails. The English fought back from galleons and smaller merchant ships hastily equipped for soldiers, and the Spanish were defeated.

Similar sailing ships were used until the nineteenth century, when steamboats were invented. Iron warships driven by steam engines began to replace sailing ships. In 1897, an English engineer named Charles Parsons built *Turbinia*, the first vessel to be driven by a steam **turbine**. This was much faster than the steamers. Soon many ships had turbine engines, including the record-breaking liner, *Mauretania*. In 1906, the British introduced a new battleship, *Dreadnought*. It had turbine engines and was armed with ten guns.

A nineteenth-century United States Navy iron warship, the U.S.S. Maine.

Until World War I, most ships burned coal to produce steam. The war brought a shortage of coal, so oil was burned instead. After the war, the first ships with motor engines began to appear.

Modern battleships are very sophisticated. They protect merchant ships and keep trade routes open; they also fight in

H.M.S. Glasgow *of the British Royal Navy is a class 42 destroyer.*

wartime. A modern fleet consists of frigates and destroyers that use electronic equipment to detect enemy ships, aircraft and submarines. Destroyers are bigger than frigates and they are armed with guns, **torpedoes** and **guided missiles**.

Small minesweepers search for **mines** under the water. Helicopters are launched from assault vessels.

The big aircraft carriers have landing decks for fighter planes to land.

Submarines travel under the water. They are driven by diesel electric engines or by **nuclear power**. Nuclear submarines can stay underwater for weeks at a time. Some nuclear-powered submarines are "hunter/killers." They are armed with torpedoes and missiles for attacking ships on the surface, and other submarines. Other, much larger submarines carry missiles that are designed to hit targets on land.

Aircraft carriers are among the biggest ships in the world. This is the U.S.S. Nimitz.

A nuclear-powered Poseidon submarine surfaces from the depths of the ocean.

The Future

Ships have certainly changed a lot since the first dugout canoe. Will they change more in the future?

These days, people have to think about saving fuel. Our oil supplies will not last forever. Designers are planning ships that make more use of the wind. This does not mean going back to sailing ships. There are plans for ships driven by wind turbines.

There are also plans for bigger and better cruise ships. For example, designers have ideas for huge "resort" ships. These would be like big hotels with harbors for water sports. They would be moored in one place for long periods of time but could be moved to find better weather or give a change of scene.

Another idea is to have ships controlled by robots. This would

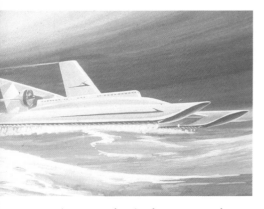

An artist's impression of a passenger ship of the future.

A futuristic design showing a high-speed hydrofoil attack ship.

save on the number of people needed to sail a fleet. There would be a "mother ship" with people on it. They would keep an eye on the robot-controlled ships in the fleet.

Designs for warships will always try to improve on speed and electronic equipment. There are plans for building submarines that can move very quietly so that they are hard to detect, and for submarines that can travel faster and operate at greater depths.

All this is a very long way from floating down a river on a log.

Glossary

Balsa A South American tree that has very soft, light wood.

Canal A water channel cut through land to join two bodies of water.

Colonies Settlements formed by groups of people in a new land.

Crude oil Oil that has not been refined into gasoline and other products.

Diesel engine An engine that burns oil and can drive heavy vehicles such as trucks and ships.

Guided missiles Weapons that can be aimed at targets that are not visible. Electronic equipment locates the enemy target and launches the missile on the right course.

Mine A type of bomb that is placed on or under the ground. Mines can also be floated on or near the surface of water, or moored on the seabed, to destroy ships.

Navigation Finding the way from one place to another.

New World The American continent, including North, South and Central America.

Nuclear power Energy produced by splitting atoms (tiny particles) of uranium. This produces great heat, which can be used to boil water and make steam to drive an engine.

Porcelain Fine china.

Torpedo A large, cigar-shaped weapon containing explosives that can travel underwater to hit its target.

Turbine An engine driven by a vaned wheel. The wheel is made to spin very fast by high-pressure jets of water, gas or steam, or by a strong wind.

Picture Acknowledgments

The illustrations in this book were supplied by: All-Sport Photographic Ltd. *cover*; The Bridgeman Art Library 10, 24; Michael Holford 12, 14, 18, 23; The Hutchison Library 4, 8, 13, 17, 20 (bottom), 21; The Illustrated London News Picture Library 19; The Mansell Collection 9 (top); The Research House 15, 20 (top), 25, 28, 29; Topham 6, 27 (bottom); Wayland Picture Library 22; ZEFA 5, 7, 16, 26, 27 (top). The artwork on pages 9 and 11 is by Richard Hook and Mark Bergin respectively.

Books to Read

Amazing Facts about Ships by Rutland. Creative Education.

Blow Ye Winds Westerly: The Seaports and Sailing Ships of Old New England by Elizabeth Gemming. Crowell Junior Books, 1972.

Columbus and the Age of Exploration by Stewart Ross. Franklin Watts (The Bookwright Press), 1985.

Ferdinand Magellan by Alan Blackwood. Franklin Watts (The Bookwright Press), 1986.

The Sea Rovers: Pirates, Privateers, and Buccaneers by Albert Martin. Atheneum, 1984.

Ships by N.S. Barrett. Franklin Watts, 1985.

Ships and Other Seacraft by Brian Williams. Franklin Watts, 1984.

Ships and Submarines by Michael Gray. Franklin Watts, 1986.

Index